THE INTELLECTUAL CASTAWAY

Joseph Raffa

The intellectual Castaway

Author: Joseph Raffa

Editor: Teena Raffa-Mulligan

ISBN 978-0-9944990-0-4

eISBN 978-0-6482503-0-2

Author's note: The term 'mankind' is used throughout this discourse in reference to the human race collectively.

Published by Sea Song Publications

sea-song@bigpond.com

www.seasongpublications.com

Contents

INTRODUCTION

FOR CENTURIES NOW, the human intellect has been expanding at a continuously accelerating rate. From small beginnings when it had only hunting, fishing, a village background and simpler techniques to draw on, it has gone through successive stages of development. Now it has a staggering accumulation of technology, experience and knowledge at its disposal.

The term intellect is used not only in this sense as the accumulated background of information, skill, expertise and memory; but also to cover the constant movement in defined directions from this accumulation to gain even further knowledge, increased comfort, greater security. Also the planning of courses of action favourable to the individual or to the nation. It operates on an individual basis to satisfy lesser demands and desires, to project ideas and also on an organised basis whereby like-minded intellects join together for a common purpose. In this way, its power to act is enhanced.

The mind relies almost totally on this extensive intellectual accumulation to determine future courses of action. The results have been enormous material benefits, a wider knowledge of our surroundings and the living of life in an organised way in which human needs are easily provided for. However, there is a destructive bent and a divisive power operating in the intellect that has not been understood, and therefore not eradicated, and the ensuing consequences over the centuries have been tragic indeed.

Should the mind continue to further its intellectual advance without uncovering its true relationship with the Universal Strangeness (the basis of all existence), the intellect will, because of the antagonisms that arise as a consequence of this lack, continue to create greater confusion, destruction and conflict, both mental and physical on an ever-increasing scale. If it persists in alienating itself from its divine source it will eventually trigger forces and pressures within and without itself that will bring it to a halt, cause it to evaluate its activity and direction and persuade it to return to the spiritual fold.

The mind, in its movement in time has created an intellectual force field to act from. This force field prevents the mind from coming into contact with others, with nature and with itself, so that the mind never approaches anything directly but only through its field of ideas, names, conclusions and memories. Operating unchallenged, the intellect has gone on gathering strength. The continual reliance by the mind on this intellectual field and the activity that arises from it, is what the mind is being asked to understand and be cautious of. The intellect, lacking the discipline of a higher directive, of any clear self-understanding is running riot. At times it has been out of control, taking mankind into uncertain, difficult and violent directions.

Whether the mind takes heed, turns away from its present courses of action and sets out to tap the spiritual resources that release the understanding to refine the intellect and control its movement, only the turn of events and the march of time will demonstrate. But this much is certain. It will turn back willingly through the arising of a spiritual understanding or it will turn back unwillingly through the ever increasing pressures of conflict and pain on every level. May the reason be the former, for if it be the latter, the years ahead are going to be increasingly disruptive.

THE INTELLECTUAL REBEL

SOMEWHERE IN THE far past, this aggressive breed of humans made their appearance, and step by step, inclination by inclination, broke away from the traditional sleepy patterns that had cast a spell over previous humans. They set out for, not subservience to nature nor harmony with nature, but complete domination, via the use of a growing intellectual prowess and the application of organised and controlled human resources.

Thrusting aside the tacit and unquestioned acceptance of faith and belief in divine forces, in the myths and magic of the past, the restless curiosity inherent in this new breed broke out of the former containing background influences. Its investigative bent surged with unrestrained momentum into every aspect of nature's appearance, into every facet of human activity. Each problem or difficulty that lined the uncertain pathway to a controlled future was reflected on, analysed and finally, when understood or thought to be so, neatly filed away in the ever growing archives of classified knowledge.

Resistance in the beginning to these new trends of inquiry and discovery was authoritatively merciless. At times, a pioneer of new learning was burnt at the stake by the fires of ignorance and fear, or tortured and forced to recant even though inwardly, those so treated were as scientifically certain of their facts as mathematical calculations and verifiable experimentation would allow. But the wheels of the new trends in thinking and discovery, once in motion, turned resolutely onwards. And as they gained momentum so the authority of the past faded, the old traditions and beliefs slowly died and a new god was born. The god of scientific certainty, of verified knowledge, whose manservant was reason, and whose council was the collective intellect of mankind. Those trained in the new ways, whatever the field, became the new experts, the new authorities whose advice was avidly sought and conscientiously adhered to whenever the need arose. The results of this applied knowledge were everywhere obvious and likewise the immense benefits that it supplied.

The scattered villages and towns of the past have been replaced with vast, complex modern cities and outer suburban centres of charm and distinctive styling in the advanced countries. Communications between cities on opposite sides of the Earth are now almost instantaneous and clear. New gadgets to tempt and arouse today's appetites and desires abound in almost every store in the technological societies. These are the present outcome of the new trends in thinking that broke the imposed shackles of the past and soared to amazing heights of creative inventiveness.

Surging like a restless river in all directions, the mind, unhindered by the restraints of faith or tradition is reaching out into every field of nature, animate and inanimate, and studying the various forms of energy, all the different life forms including its own. It is constantly searching, experimenting, probing in its never-ending quest to make its control of life and the environment as complete as humanly possible. The inhibitions of the past crumbled rapidly. So too did any semblance of induced stability that was largely the result of an unquestioned acceptance of the prevailing authorities in religion and learning, and the domination of traditional ideas in living.

The accepted values disintegrated one by one, swept aside by the energetic onslaught of the human intellect on the march in time, eager to plant its flag of conquest on the highest pinnacle of truthful discovery. It became much more difficult for people to create a sure and stable base out of religious, moral, social and political ideas to support them through the rapid changes that followed as a consequence of this intellectual stretching of wings by mankind. Now, in the full flight of its activity, the constant arising of new ideas is the fledgling created by the thrust and force of the intellect at work and play in the accustomed playground of time.

Here, it seems that no bounds have been set on the discoveries the intellect can make, nor on the directions it travels in its search for new ideas and experiences, or in its efforts to understand deeper its own nature and the nature of the surrounding universe. The instruments at its disposal are marvels of scientific engineering and creative genius. These too are the result of the intellectual capacity of mankind working methodically in this direction.

So we have come to the present stage in human development. The intellect due to its many discoveries and the application of these discoveries for the improvement of the health and wellbeing of humanity is being hailed as the only worthwhile God, to be faithfully worshipped and listened to with reverence. With such tremendous results accrued after centuries of application, how then can the position of the intellect be challenged and particularly its manservant reason, without seeming to be foolish in the extreme?

We cannot deny the achievements in so many fields. We cannot deny the improvements that we daily take for granted. Materially, scientifically, educationally, agriculturally: in arts, crafts, amusements and whatever else we may have, use or do, we have gained so much and our lives may now be very comfortable indeed. We are surrounded in the industrialised countries with a great deal of luxury living. And the underdeveloped countries are doing their best to achieve the same levels of development.

Technologically, there is no standing still. The intellect continues to move on with breathtaking speed. With the atom harnessed, new sources of energy became available and so too did deadlier and more destructive bombs. Paralleling the inventive genius of the intellect is a hellish inventiveness for the ultimate in weapons of destruction. Complex weapon systems to operate from ground, sea or air bristle like formidable porcupine quills from well concealed hideouts. Banks of electronic computers with ever busy circuits amass, record and digest data to feed fear ridden intellects with information that may protect the security of the insecure and reassure the fearful. Hidden deep in the labyrinths of intellectual activity, a cunning and diabolical reason, with deadly efficiency, entraps the inventive genius of mankind and directs it towards malignant and destructive ends.

Lurking like a diseased sewer rat, swollen fat with the blood of humans — ever hungry for more — with an insatiable appetite for blood, misery, suffering and pain, a deranged intellect is on the rampage in time. Its cunning has been honed by centuries of experience in the art of destruction. Its camouflage is highly perfected after generations of practice in deceit and masterly covering up. Its reason has been forged by the fires of fear and the heat of a multitude of urges and desires into a barrage of formidable offensive and defensive verbal rockets.

Such are the subterfuges and processes employed to serve the changing moods of the intellectual monster. This monster, with its amazing ability to split itself up into many strong, independent and opposing centres — which are really different groups of various ideas, attitudes and accepted standpoints and lifestyles — has divided and subdivided the vast populations of this planet into separatist groups, organisations, nations and religions, each one continually in opposition with others, sometimes to the point of destructive conflict.

The intellectual monster thrives on conflict and dissension, on differences, discord, fear and suspicion. These situations and reactions, once they arise between humans, set the means for the monster to flex its intellectual muscles and move to the forefront of the human stage wherein the drama of human living is enacted with all its terrifying futility, pathos and despair. Here, with a command of oratory that is flexible, practised, persuasive, logically convincing and deceitful, the multi-headed intellect, operating on many fronts at the same instant in time, acts to continue the dispersion of the human race. A dispersion that began thousands of years ago and one that has intensified steadily and inexorably. Today, humans no longer recognise the hidden bond of universal brotherhood, nor the divine Universal

Strangeness that is the reality behind this unified brotherhood.

THE UNKNOWING INTELLECT

STRANGE BUT TRUE, no awareness of this divine being has yet penetrated the consciousness of millions of people. There is a blankness within the human entity that many humans have yet to explore. They pay a great deal of attention to the outer world. There is awareness of the body, feelings and thinking processes. But beyond this, an impenetrable barrier seems to have settled in, one that has effectively cut people off from the very essence of what they are.

Embedded deep within the human being as its life source is a nature shrouded in mystery and one that is difficult to realise. It lies beyond the dead extent that humans have allowed to develop within the mind. If humans would cross this cemetery of the dead — this inner graveyard of memories, ideas, thoughts, attitudes, fears and desires, this conglomeration of knowledge and experience that is the ego's lifeblood and attracts the total attention of the mind — they would come to an enchanting universal sensitivity full of richness and wonder. And they would profit immensely from the new depth of understanding released.

Human living cannot flourish if there is no awakening to this inner side, if life goes on without any deep awareness of its existence and relationship to the surface self. The resources within this unknown side are of immense value to the surface self. The understanding released when integration happens is superior to that attained by intellectual reason through its own efforts. The sense of wellbeing that flows in is so uplifting and not affected by surface conditions operating at the time. The release from struggle, effort and tension affects every aspect of the surface personality and the human expression sparkles inwardly like the springtime in full bloom. The redirection given to day to day living in whatever we undertake is empowered by the light of TRUTH and takes us on the pathway of peace and harmony.

We live with greater care and move confidently in time without undue concerns. Our steps are clear, we know where we are at and what we belong to. All the alternative lifestyles contending for attention in the marketplace of time, where modern spruikers eager to gain adherents ply their wares to entice the unwary, are understood to be byways along which people travel only to reach the proverbial dead end. The ultimate that life has to offer is discovered not in time, nor in experience no matter how deeply sought, but beyond in that timeless expanse that is the mind's very own essence. This is the source from whence it arose out of shrouded mystery to crystalise its effects and actions so clearly in the accustomed world of space and time.

Because humans are not living fully in the spiritual strangeness, a fracture has developed and widened. With reckless speed the intellect is pouring its undisciplined attention and energy into time, giving free rein to the ideas that arise and using its drive to build and shape society along the lines laid down. These are fashioned from experience as ideas prove their effectiveness and by the commanding desires, attitudes and intentions operating through every intellect involved in organisation, whether at the bottom of the tree of authority or at the top.

The intellect does not operate impartially in its search for new ideas to benefit mankind unless it be under the guidance of the inner spiritual directive. Even should the ideas implemented be experimentally verifiable and thoroughly tested as to their effects, the benefits to mankind may become controlled by greed or by the power hungry. As long as influences are at work in the intellect that are not selfless and altruistic it cannot create a world in which harmony, peace and enough for all is the norm. If there is fear, it pulls towards the protection of fear, greed moves towards the furtherance of greed and uncertainty as a base for action instead of the clear light of TRUTH leads to further uncertainty.

Only the clear understanding released by a dawning spirituality can direct humanity through the difficult problems and situations arising so rapidly and threatening to overwhelm us today. The problems, the situations, are the direct result of the stampeding intellect as it gallops out of control, out of touch with its spiritual essence. With reason as the rider it has galloped in every direction that time and experience has offered and which seemingly promise discoveries of great value. Cascading in the wake of its travel are the technological discoveries and inventions we use today. Arts, crafts, entertainments, new designs for cities, all these have broken away from their past slowly altering base and now change is skyrocketing along in all directions and affecting humans in most everything they do.

We have now become so deeply embedded in the momentum of the intellect's movement that we are incapable of applying the brakes and pausing to evaluate the directions of its many thrusts, nor the underlying motivations that control the use of its discoveries and the further direction of its flow. It has dug deep into every surface facet of nature's appearance. The atom has yielded many of its secrets and so too have the arrangements of genes that provide the fundamental basis for life to express its creative force. Never satisfied, never still, the motto of the intellect is onwards, regardless of consequences. Directing the flow of nature's energy from one form to another, rearranging natural resources, controlling and moulding the growth and end result of living forms to suit its own ideas or needs — all this the intellect would continually strive for, till its control of nature's domain, both animate and inanimate, was authoritatively absolute. Provided of course, such an absolute control is possible. As yet, the intellect does not acknowledge many limits except those of limited experience and lack of time, and it expects to have unhindered access to both with the continuing passage of time and the growing accumulation of experience.

How long will the undisciplined movement of the intellect continue before mankind awakens to the danger this poses? If the inner High Control does not assert itself to control the intellect of mankind through love and understanding, where will it take mankind? Already tremendously destructive weapons are available, and perhaps only fear of like retaliation prevents their use.

So many problems have come in the wake of the intellect's discoveries and application. Environmental damage and pollution, unbalanced development, dictatorships imposed due to the use of the weapons invented, people grappling to fit into the rapidly changing technological societies, medicine and chemicals hailed as boons at the time of discovery then found to be dangerous with the passing of time. All these difficulties have been created by the rapid strides of the intellect and are now passed on to the specialists to solve — again by the use of the intellect's reasoning prowess and capacity to understand.

So whatever the field, the problems created by the intellect are passed on to another intellectual department to solve, while humanity goes on its way to further new discoveries and increasingly more complex lifestyles that promise improved quality, greater prosperity and more security and comfort.

That is, if no destructive conflicts arise to shatter the sweet dreams of the drifting intellect as it busies itself about its daily business.

And sometimes grave disturbances do challenge the arrogant intellect's confidence in its own ability to neatly lay out patterns of living to handle every emerging contingency. Very deep social divisions plague the nations of the world today. There isn't any area that the intellect isn't involved with that reflects total harmony, whether political, scientific, religious, national, or any other activity. And this applies just as obviously to individual living. There are storms to the right, antagonisms to the left, divisions in the centre, and troubles all around — all created by intellectual thinking that has broken loose from the masterly control and love of the unknown inner nature of mankind.

There is no divine illumination operating to redirect the intellectual's direction simply because the intellect denies the need of and the reality of the divine strangeness that is the secret source of its existence. Feeling self-contained and unchallenged except by opposing intellects and having no direct evidence of the Universal Oneness that is its true nature, the mind of man limits itself to the reasoned conclusions and ideas of the self-created intellect. It acts out its life and directs its energies in total disregard of the importance of this inner nature to its own wellbeing and even to its continued existence on this planet.

For the pendulum that swings between destruction and harmony is a finely balanced one. The weight of the intellect's activity towards disruption is slowly gaining momentum and inexorably the pendulum is pointing towards this end. Yet, as a counter balance there is a movement back to the spiritual homeland by the more perceptive. But if the momentum towards disruption is allowed to go too far, nothing can prevent the disastrous results from engulfing mankind. The imbalance caused by the intellect's blindness must be redressed by an outpouring of what it is capable of. It is like the stresses and strains beneath the earth that presage an earthquake. Meanwhile in the wake of the pendulum's swing, increasing tensions of various kinds are straining the social fabric in many places.

Alarmed at the results of its own incompetence, for which it does not yet accept full responsibility, the intellect, stirred by the magnitude of the surrounding problems and concerned with the constant threat to its many achievements, has marshalled its resources world-wide to tackle the difficulties on an international scale. The finest intellects from the four corners of the Earth and in between meet often to deal with the many difficulties that confront them. They reason logically, make suggestions, pass legislation, lobby for support amongst nations. Yet still, in spite of the most dedicated efforts very little has been accomplished in the creation of harmony and goodwill. And the same serious divisions still threaten to disrupt the establishment of real peace on Earth. That is, a true peace that we have had as yet no memory of, nor one that seems likely to eventuate in the very near future.

Why is it that the collective intellect of mankind which has uncovered a mass of facts and created so much of benefit to humanity always seems to bog down when it comes to what is fundamentally of the greatest importance? And that is the creation of harmony, peace, goodwill — all the qualities humans hunger for and rarely seem to enjoy without interruption. Could it be that peace and harmony are not the result of intellectual processes and that these desirable states of wellbeing are beyond its intellectual skill to produce and maintain?

If we observe the intellect in action, what is obvious is that it strives for acceptable conclusions that are the result of its own logical processes working along avenues to satisfy the ambitions, desires and attachments of the self. Its interest is in conclusions which meet its deepest demands and allow an outlet of its wants unhindered by rival or contrary claims. The intellect never operates in a vacuum. It draws from a complex background whose roots often go back centuries in time. Even so-called revolutionary intellects do not break completely with the past. If they did they would have little to draw on, and what would they use to control and manage society while they were educating others along what they insist is something totally new? They too, in some ways are instruments of the past and thereby an extension of the influential background the intellect draws on.

If we are to understand how the intellect operates, we must explore this accumulation it uses as its operating base. Everyone has a base of some kind. It is the lifeblood of the intellectual approach and should it be cut off from this base for prolonged periods it would be starved of sustenance and not operate too effectively. This is why true change (spiritual) when it does happen, comes slowly so the intellect can gradually assimilate the insights that come its way. Too radical a change alarms the intellect, which only feels comfortable amongst its familiar and accustomed patterns of thinking and acting. And it is these accustomed patterns of thinking, to a large extent inherited from the past, from the adopted background pool, that project the ugly divisions and problems existing today. Rather unrealistically, we attempt to solve these disturbing situations by the use of the very same processes.

Today's problems — all the ugly behaviour spreading like a dark cloud over the planet, striking now here, now there — is not just an accidental arising. The top intellects in every nation are constantly at work devising ways and means to cope with the mounting pressures and tensions. The resources used (reason and accumulated experience) must in some way be limited to produce such disruptive effects. If the limited manner in which the intellect approaches problems is not clearly understood it will continue to inflame the arising situations. The attention of experts has failed to clear away the mounting tide of disarray that spills out with such tragic impact where conflict holds sway.

Humanity has yet to realise that the only responsible role in life for the intellect is to be the servant of a higher love and revelatory understanding. This refines and disciplines the intellect of its inherent weaknesses, its self-centred obsessions and its capacity for false perceptions based on its acceptance of separation as a fact of life; and the denial of Oneness, of a unified state that is the only and true nature of all mankind — indeed of all life and manifest existence. When it has yielded its position of sovereignty and blended with the universal, it is motivated in its movement by a new level of understanding based on universal truths and not on self-centred bias. It is guided by a quality of love and a deep consideration that will not permit it to be used against its fellow intellects for any sinister or self-centred purpose whatsoever.

In the meantime, running riot in timeland as it does, creating all kinds of mischief and friction, it is slowly coming to a confrontation with the diabolical in itself. Should this happen because of its continued blindness in traveling along its present misaligned path, there is likely to be much in the way of torment and turmoil. And, in the hall of the impersonal justice that rules at the heart of things, the finger of blame will point directly at this arrogant upstart, this rebellious perverter of its station in life, which from a small beginning grew into a monstrous threat to itself, to others and to its environment.

CAN THE INTELLECT AWAKEN?

T HERE COMES A time during the intellect's sojourn on Earth when the suggestion to return to its spiritual home begins to bear fruit. The intellect, for a complex of reasons dedicates itself to this grand involvement. It is intrigued by this offering of a unique nature that has neither appearance nor form, that even the process of thinking cannot grasp. The intellect, according to the degree of interest shown, gathers its energy and talents to tackle this new and exciting undertaking. Not having any experience to guide it, it turns to those who seemingly offer guidance towards this unknown dimension.

Some stay anchored in the study of sacred books. They rely on the recorded sayings of divinely inspired men and women of the past. Their interest is partly satisfied by an intellectual understanding of what has been recorded. Others, impatient to realise in the present lifetime the reality of this one and only universal nature, turn to those who are living exponents of this nature — the awakened ones.

For the intellects that are inwardly ripe for this great adventure it is usually the case that they come into personal contact with one who has been through it all. This may be effected through the written word. Being inwardly ready for this journey towards The Silent Heart, they sense the importance of what they are being offered. So the stage is set for the intellect's involvement with the fullness of what life has to offer.

In the early stages of this quest, unsure of itself and how to proceed, the intellect reaches out for guidelines and support, for reassurance that it is heading in the right direction. This reaction is understandable but too strong a desire for projected avenues leaves the intellect open to offerings that keep it functioning and enclosed in a maze of protracted self-effort — in effect, a self-created prison. However, not to give the intellect something to proceed with would leave it dangling in mid-air, eager to move but with no place to go. To serve this need to have something to aim at, systems of reflection, mental exercises and forms of meditation have been devised to absorb the intellect's attention and to encourage it to continue with its endeavours in this new direction of exploring within.

Discussions with those who are clear lights or the reading of their books helps to clear the mental air somewhat and give sound ideas on what is involved. As the intellect continues its explorations, spearheaded by reasonable investigations, it gradually exhausts whatever means it is using without any encouraging results, although meditations may bring useful benefits. To the thoughtful intellect it may become obvious after long periods of unproductive effort that it does not know what it is after; and that through a continuation of effort, no matter how persistent, it cannot proceed on sure steps into this new direction.

No amount of explanation yields the necessary understanding to dispel ignorance while the mental barriers that prevent realisation are still in place. Self-understanding requires great care by the intellect, for such is the nature of thought and its eagerness for quick results that it may create the illusion of progress, or returns that are not really valid or truthful. The intellect will come to anchor in the field of self-satisfaction with techniques and self-involvement of one kind or another till a rising tide of discontent forces it to re-evaluate its position and acknowledge it has discovered nothing new.

The seeking intellect continues its involvement with techniques, self-analysis, meditation or whatever till it exhausts these avenues and burns out the illusion that these are the bridges that lead to spiritual discovery. Self-application is important in the beginning because if it does not question experience, life, the mind and everything going on within and without, the intellect remains sound asleep. And to those who are asleep in time, realisation of the one nature that pervades all cannot happen. Yet it is also true that if the intellect persists in seeking its own answers to its insistent questions using the means of reasonable thought leading to acceptable thought-out conclusions, it will not go beyond this but remain on this level.

That which is referred to as the Oneness is not a thought-out conclusion which is the outcome of intellectual activity, is created by and supposedly understood by the intellect. Mental conclusions are its offspring, born of its bent in this direction and sustained by its understanding — one that has many inherent limitations. The process of thought is limited by the perceptions of the intellect, by the incapacity of thinking to go beyond its boundaries. It must produce results it can understand, and in as much that the intellect's approach is from a supposedly separate standpoint and deals with fragments and sections rather than grasping the totality, the results are often contradictory — acceptable today, denied tomorrow.

The realisation of the underlying Oneness is not brought about by intellectual understanding operating under the auspices of reason and self-intention. Regardless of whether there is awareness of the universal or not, its existence continues. The surging intellectual movement, no matter how insistent, cannot penetrate into this dimension. The intellect is birthed in time, sharpens its wits on the whetstone of time and knows itself through the experiences of time. This is its field of work and play. It can arrange and rearrange, learn and unlearn, juggle thoughts endlessly and weave these into a satisfactory pattern that represents its level of understanding about itself and the universe. Through its reasonable endeavours it hopes to unravel the mysteries of nature including its own.

In whatever fields it is active in, it sets up systems of checks and counterchecks to verify every step taken, carefully evaluating every experience as to its worth and meaning. Self-protection from error is the keynote of its endeavours and its level of understanding is the measure by which it verifies its conclusions on the scales of experience. It makes self-conscious living possible and we haven't yet learned to carry on without its constant activity. It is the means through which we comprehend the phenomenal world. Everything humans come into contact with travels through the computer of the intellect, which automatically selects, digests, judges and records for future use the results of its own inspection.

The intellect is an activity born of the mind's movement in the field of time. Intelligible to the mind, it is the only language it knows until something else comes along. To ask the self to cease its intellectual utterances (with speech as the outer expression and thought as the inner) would be like cutting the tongue out and then trying to talk. Without this accustomed activity it would be lost and unable to communicate. The mind has never known itself to be without this noisy companion except during deep sleep: now it has become second nature for the mind to respond in this way.

In fact, the mind sees intellectual expression as its most valued expression. It feeds the expression constantly, studying, learning, observing so that it can accumulate a more skilful and versatile base for the intellect to operate and communicate from. Logic, the art of reasoning well has been devised to present undeniable and persuasive conclusions. The intellect thrives in the use of logical expertise as a means to confront and question life and experience, to define difficulties and problems and deliver satisfactory answers.

And yet the highest nature of all, the universal reality that reflects itself in life and the universe lies beyond the grasp of intellectual reason. Without tangible evidence of some kind the intellect has nothing to focus on so it passes on to dwell in what it is familiar with. The intellect is above all a very reasonable movement. It considers that what it cannot observe is not worth the time of the day or of not much use anyway. It thrives on the use of reason and in fact to keep things on a reasonable level suits it fine. Reason has been developed as a means of investigation and communication. Mind feels at home with this and values it highly.

To suggest there is a universal nature beyond the scope of reason as initiated by the self from its limited level of understanding is somewhat frustrating to a reason that urges to know the what, why and where of everything. Yet what processes of thought can be projected to uncover the universal nature that presents no tangible qualities for thought to apprehend? And without evidence of some kind, how is the nature of the universal confirmed within the mind?

The constant intellectual flow, be it thinking, reason or whatever else falls within the orbit of the observable draws the attention down to the identifiable and the knowable. Awareness is locked in to a perception of the outer and a redirection of the attention is not possible while this is ongoing. Reliant on the intellect to dispel confusion and doubt, to clear the way ahead, unknowing of revelatory resources contained within, the mind places the intellect with its commander in chief — reason — on a pedestal of importance. It proceeds to go to sleep and allow the intellect to take over its approach to life. And because an intellect focused on the outer, bedevilled with concepts of separation, not knowing the underlying Oneness that pervades all, is riddled with false perception and ingrained ignorance, it creates divisions amongst humans where none exist and disorder instead of harmony and cooperation.

It is difficult for the intellect to yield the position of top authority it has long enjoyed. Flash floods of a revelatory understanding are needed from time to time to break the intellect's hold and force it to abdicate its position. Its stubbornness to hold on is remarkable in depth, tenacity and durability. Its resistance is only broken by the advent of Love, by influxes of understanding from a higher level that intervene to give a helping hand when the seeking self in its guise of the intellect bogs down with the realisation it cannot go beyond its limits through its own efforts. Now, by the light of clearly arising truth it can see how it created problems and bound itself by limited perception in its endeavours to discover the universal.

The separate standing of the self was only a false concept created by intellectual thought through the persuasive power of the senses and the distinctive presentation of the phenomenal world. From this basic flaw in its approach, the intellect fashioned an edifice of understanding that was fragmentary in its approach and denied any arising of what is fundamentally true about human nature and its relationship with the universal. By this new light it learns the universal is not intellectual in nature, cannot be understood by this means and lies forever outside the probing proboscis of the intellectual elephant that rampages across the sensitivity we refer to as the mind.

THE LIMITED INTELLECT

T IS SOMEWHAT disconcerting to say to an intellect full of technological discoveries and achievements in many fields that its scope is limited when it comes to investigating the deeper levels of the human expression. Effects that lodge in the conscious are recorded by the intellectual register and acknowledged as evidence of what is happening in the extent of the unconscious. Where nothing registers to arouse intellectual interest, no movement takes place to gain new knowledge and deepen the understanding. The intellect must, by the nature of what it is, deal with that which offers some kind of tangible evidence of its existence.

Matters of the occult, the spiritual, the extra sensory are difficult to verify experimentally and, not being open to humans in the same way that external phenomena is, remain somewhat of an enigma to the exploring intellect. It has been rather lately that science has moved to explore what is referred to as the psychic field and the mood is one of proceed with caution seeing the evidence is not easily verifiable by a large cross section of observers. The science intellect is more at ease checking with instruments and using the consensus of reason, and it accepts with a sense of relief what falls within the universal laws it has discovered and is accustomed to.

Ingenious instruments are the expanded eyes and ears of the investigating intellect. These are the vanguard of its attempts to understand deeper the mysteries of life and the universe. Any unusual experiences that unfold and the science intellect comes to the party with its baggage of complex instruments. They are its gateway to a wider knowledge and it considers instruments the bridge to travel along to learn the ultimate secrets of life.

But here is the paradox — instruments need a focus as does the mind of man. They can only discern what they have been programmed to discern. Beyond the designed function they cannot go. So much of the phenomenal world may be examined in this way but this is the outer movement of a creative process that has its inception on a deeper level, one beyond the scope of both instruments and intellectual vision.

How do you record the quality of perception, the dawn of understanding, the release of insights, the nature of love? What can be observed on the surface is just one part of the story —the other, the universal side and what goes on in the unconscious is hidden from the prying eyes of the intellect while it holds to its separatist standpoint. And if the existence of a higher realm as the source of all cannot be verified through complex techniques and logical reason, how is this to happen? Humans will not pay homage forever to a phantom that does not offer any concrete evidence of its existence nor demonstrate its value in the only way this is acceptable — by direct experience and a definite improvement in the human condition.

Fortunately humans have the means to make their way back to the mystery of what I refer to as the spiritual strangeness, (the source of all that is manifest and known). The seeker will have to put aside instruments and the acquired knowledge of the intellect. Reason will need to be disciplined to stay within its boundaries and not try to venture beyond on a mission that is doomed to failure. Reason in full flight remains on the level of thought and thoughtful conclusions. This is inevitable, that's its nature.

Within the net of reason, only the known can be entangled. But the ultimate cannot be trapped in this way. It is timeless, spaceless, without form and void. The intellect belongs to time. Here, it has a ball. There is much to examine, to investigate, to reflect on and think about. So many variable bits and pieces on show. For the discovery of the ultimate, time's flowing movement must come to a standstill. With no movement in time, so the intellect fades out of the picture. It cannot exist when the universe is still, when thought, feeling and sensation are still. There is nothing to rouse it, to feed its appetite, to spur its movement to express thoughts.

In time, mind is concerned with a myriad sensations, with the ebb and flow of experience, with the constant movement of thought. This is the dance of time, an impressive show that holds the intellect tuned in with time. Here, the observed and the observer hold sway as seemingly separate phenomena. On this side of time's great divide there is no evidence of the totality, of the universal strangeness, and the intellect parades as the only directive that matters. It is difficult for an intellect steeped in timeful display to step aside and let this display come to a brief end so that silence reigns unbroken. Action from thought will not bring this about. Any movement from the intellect to help is only a hindrance and keeps the artificial division between the observer and the observed ongoing. What to do? See the uselessness of action from the self — just see. Let the inner focus maintain itself without resorting to time-fashioned movement whatever this is.

A revelatory upsurge of understanding is the prerequisite for freeing the inner sensitivity from the dominance of time. It happens without preparation when all the conditions are ripe for it. Let go, don't hold to the past, to thought, to known influences. This is what stymies the intellect. It cannot get in on the action, prepare the ground and control the show. Let it understand this and not interfere. It takes only a moment for Oneness to take over and that is enough to clear the mind of confusion and demonstrate to the intellect what an interfering busybody it is. Then when it's over, time's impressive display comes crowding back in, filling the surface mind with its strident cacophony and the urgent voices of desire, of needs, and demands call out again, begging for attention. So too does the intellect take off again. But there has been a change in understanding and this begins to project its influence.

The so-called avenue and the means that allow the discovery of the universal strangeness to happen cannot be clearly conveyed intellectually. Descriptions are a reflection of the intellect's nature, are initiated in time where the intellect surveys its handiwork. In the garden of time, the intellect is at home tending the plants of ideas, shaping these as it will, accepting and rejecting as it works. Such a busy worker and here it performs very well indeed. But in the discovery of the universal strangeness it must keep its intellectual nose out of the way. Its business is to ask the initial questions and demonstrate its willingness to learn. With its admirable capacity for precise logic it clears the air to a certain extent by defining possibilities and discarding illogical conclusions. When it has reached the limits of thinking (and it is a sign of maturity when it realises this) it must back off and allow the inner nature to demonstrate what it alone can do.

When this happens, the magnitude of the revelation is such that the intellect sees its former high opinion of its worth was very much overrated. The intellect arrives at this point sooner or later. If it has not exhausted every avenue at its disposal, examined every byway it moves along, every crutch it uses for support, it will not yield in its intentions to carry on through its own efforts. It will hold on, establishing itself in some tangible way in the course of its investigations to discover the meaning of life and its relationship with the universal reality. If its driving interest is such that it must discover the truth and nothing but the truth about the meaning of existence, it will continue until it exhausts every means without success. It may not understand why this must be so but still, at such an instant when it is ready to let go, it is on the brink of allowing the conditions to be just what they should be for the Grand Awakening to happen of its own accord.

The intellect, exhausted, with no place to go, with its momentum burnt out by the frustrating lack of success, comes to a standstill, no longer willing to be intellectually involved any more. It has reached the end of the intellectual line. No more thought-created stations arise to tempt it into further action.

But the interest to discover is still there, deep and abiding. An inner demand that will not be denied. This too must vanish. As long as it continues it will disturb the conscious mind and the intellect may respond, stir into action and try to deal with it. The stillness must be deeper than an intellectual one.

The inner too must be free of any stresses and strains. Absolute stillness, then, is the prerequisite of spiritual discovery, unknown, complete and original.

No more effort by the mind to be involved in any of the ways open to it. Intellectual thinking non-existent. Desires, demands, driving interest and discontent all come to rest in a state where there is no breakaway movement from the primal state of being. The impulse towards sensation, feeling is also temporarily stilled. Only the background sensitivity exists now. Universal silence has taken over and absorbed the vast scattering of the manifest universe. This then is the only way to go, to be One with the Great One. Put aside the tide of the known, all of it, including the intellectual outpouring: out it goes, all of it with the debris, the flotsam and jetsam from time's movement that has impinged within and cluttered up the inner side.

Don't worry, you will not disintegrate nor be destroyed. You will be reborn in truth as well as spiritually. The awakening will flood through and revitalise you. There may be excitement and ecstasy but these pass, leaving you with an unshakeable certainty of what you are, of what you share in a Oneness with the Universal Nature. The first moment is only the beginning of a new learning. You still have far to go but from now on you will not be so reliant on the capacity of the intellect to take you forward as a reliable guide as you were formerly. You begin to walk now on the spiritual side of life; the directive is the moments when Oneness reigns. And this will carry you forward, surely and clearly according to how deeply you understand the ego and put it aside, whatever its ramifications.

THE INTELLECT CONCEDES

THE INTELLECT THAT began in such a hurry to place its individual stamp all over the face of life served its purpose in the movement towards the Universal Reality when it carried the mind to the limits of its understanding. It served even further when it pulled its intellectual head in, when it realised it could no longer add anything of value in the way of intelligent guidelines or true answers to the what, where and why of life and God. As a consequence of the discovery of its relationship with the universal, it finds itself in an uncertain position as to its role in the human expression.

Somewhat put out that the discovery arises through the advent of grace rather than through its own involved approach, it sets to, after it has regained its balance, to remould its approach. It absorbs the new experiences into its former accumulated base, which is not lost but reactivated via memory when the intellect returns to its customary role in time. Slowly, as the effects of the initial discovery fade the intellect gradually reasserts itself and begins again to dominate the human expression. With its gradual re-emergence as ruler of the kingdom of the mind, the light that brightly shone at the moment of discovery and the illuminating aftermath fade away.

The intellect is left to do what it will with the new learning that has come its way. There is wisdom in this. The arrogance of the intellect is bent but not broken by one burst of illumination. For sure it sees much at that moment. But it has yet to learn of its capacity for change, the way it responds to renew its former patterns of behaviour. It takes many an influx of spiritual understanding, spread over many years of experience, to yield the full story of the intellect's devious ways. With each burst that follows that first moment of revelation the intellect is allowed full rein to re-establish its movement and to operate at will to its own advantage with the learning gained. In this way, as the learning proceeds, the intellect becomes more deeply aware of its ingrained limitations and self-centred obsession.

The understanding released by spiritual contact, by union with the universal nature, is of a higher level than the normal one. There is no self-motivation or manipulation involved. Behind the thrust of intellectual activity there are many motivations, each expressing an intention to serve the expectations, demands and desires of the personal self. They mould the exploring bent of the intellect, confining its energetic forays into a self-contained orbit. Service of the self, one way or another is the over-riding demand imposed on the intellectual flow. Discipline itself as it will to avoid this, only a deep understanding of the deceptive power of thought prevents misconceptions from arising. And the power of the intellectual self to persist along avenues of its choosing is only shattered by the insights released when revelation sweeps away the blindness that has long held sway.

The intellect, lacking illumination, has become the disciple for disorder and disarray. It has also sought to eliminate any acknowledgement of a divine nature in its equations. Reliant on its own capacity to make its way, the consequences have been unbalanced. Brilliant technological advances, useful organisations, but so much that is displeasing in human behaviour. The intellect insists on being top dog, not subservient to any other power except its own logical expertise.

The advent of spiritual moments in which it is non-existent as an individual movement puts a temporary dent in its accustomed standing. It cannot deny what has happened nor the input of the fresh understanding that follows. But it finds it difficult to step aside, to accept relegation to a lesser role, to one of being a servant between what is a higher nature and its own lesser role in the human expression.

Denying its spiritual heritage, the intellect has taken over to lead mankind where it will. From a surface standpoint it seems that it can travel along its own predetermined pathways with little interference. It is not unduly disturbed by small wars here and there, industrial unrest, widespread starvation or economic variations. The intellect is in a sleepy state of rolling along with the tide of events it has created. It does not realise what may lie ahead but the evidence is there for the discerning ones whose intellectual heads are not buried ostrich like in the busy tide of social events.

There is still a vast array of destructive weapons scattered worldwide, including atomic weapons ready for use. There are widespread environmental problems, social, economic, international and religious differences. The young are discontented, turning away from former values and looking in other directions for a way out of their disenchantment. Violence in many forms waxes and wanes, people are often afraid to venture out nights and many homes have become fortresses of fear with an array of protective devices.

It is a topsy turvy world yet day by day the status quo is accepted and ordinary people feel that personally they can do very little about it. They rely for change on the political intellect, on an array of expert talent. But whatever approach the intellect uses based on its reasonable initiatives, the human race keeps heading for a showdown, a confrontation with all the intellect is capable of. What will it take to awaken the human race, to disturb the intellect so profoundly that it alters course, turns away from its energetic momentum towards disorder and begins to listen to the whispers from within, from a higher directive?

All the agony of wars, of messy troubles in between — none of this has yet led to a worldwide awakening of the right kind: a spiritual one. Individuals do not want to stir and help themselves climb out of their blindness and ignorance of their spiritual connection. They prefer to leave their security and wellbeing in the intellectual hands that have wrought so much destruction, disorder and emotional and mental imbalance. What nature brings in the way of earthquakes, floods and droughts and natural disasters, all these we may not yet be able to do much about. But the damage done by greed, blindness, prejudice, selfishness and the like, operating unhindered in the grasping, fear-ridden world of today we can certainly do without — and must if humans are to flourish.

How much closer will the intellect take mankind to the point of no return? Always the battlefield of destruction is waiting, its gates wide open. Intellectual arrogance prepares the entrance and from time to time and in spite of technological brilliance, the intellect rushes in to experience widespread slaughter and mental and emotional agony. It is little use crying out for help when the momentum for disruption goes too far. Talking threats, thinking aggressively, inclinations for violence generate their own movements.

Energy directed towards aggressive behaviour must run its course. Change its course as it will, the intellect, without reconnection with the spiritual, without the love and understanding this brings, must perforce carry on from the background pool of self-centred inclinations it has nurtured for generations. This is the conditioning influence that has been responsible for the confusion, the conflict, the mayhem that have been the intellect's constant companions over the years.

Human nature reflects in the mirror of life everything it is capable of. In the outer world it sees the results of its inner handiwork. Looking at the outer reflection through self-prejudiced eyes, the intellect distorts the truth about its own contribution. It is a master at this kind of deception and it has cultivated the art of covering up ever since its inception as the protector of the self's position in life. In fact, so skilful is the camouflage painted over by the intellect that it defies the capacity of logical reason to expose it once the power of self-delusion is deeply entrenched in the mind.

Only a spiritual stripper of exceptional quality can lay bare the sinister and devious controlling influences that direct the intellect along self-centred, limited pathways of travel. Surprisingly, without being aware of the subtle control exercised by self-manipulation based on the desire to expand, enhance and protect the standing of the self, the intellect considers it has freely chosen to proceed after the utmost consideration of all the factors involved. The spiritual stripper is available, deep within the human content, and when its cleansing action has been applied to the grasping intellect an astonishing change in understanding takes place. The covering overlay of adopted attitudes, the thought processes that operate to protect the self's base of ideas, its projections, possessions and whatever else it maintains for its own purposes are momentarily dissolved by the influx of a super charged insight of exceptional clarity.

With the overlying deceptions removed, mind is aglow with a penetrating light. Mind is this light. It shines through unhindered. Intellectual clutter has been removed, its distortive tendencies temporarily terminated. Now the intellect can see how it had allowed itself to be controlled and manipulated, not only by its own desires, fears and personal inclinations but also by others, by national, religious, political influences — the whole kit and caboodle of the social collective past. All this past input has been digging in deeper and deeper, enslaving the intellect, directing it to move in further support of the prevailing established accumulation. As long as this continues the intellect is in chains, manipulated to move like a puppet on the stage of time with the controlling strings hidden out of intellectual sight in the unconscious extent of the mind.

It is difficult for the intellect to break out into the freedom of the spiritual while so firmly bound in this way. It takes a deep and persistent longing to be free of all restraints, even of the movement of intellectual thought to even challenge this self-imposed bondage. The intellect motors its way over the surface extent of life. What lies below the surface view is difficult to investigate, particularly to thought processes that belong to a surface expression. What to do then? We are not only what is observed outwardly, and although the existence of the so-called unconscious and its capacity to influence behaviour is recognised, into this level the intellect cannot directly go and maintain its customary standing as an intellectual movement.

The constant thrust by the intellect to gain control and intellectual understanding limits the mind and channels the surface self to a narrow intellectual focus. Always seeking intellectual answers to intellectual questions, it goes its intellectual way mesmerised by the sound of its own thinking, lulled to sleep by the soothing sound of thoughts washing across the surface of the mind. They are familiar friends, always welcome. Should they not be there for any span of conscious time, thought responds to fill the vacuum.

This is partly why the mind is active intellectually — it cannot bear the seeming vacuum when it ceases intellectual activity for a time. It has rowed the intellectual boat, fast or slow, erratic or steady since it first learned the art of applying itself in this way. This is its own language and it cannot bear to be without it. Intellect communicates to other intellects via the means of thought and it keeps itself company when alone by thinking to itself, sorting out problems, making decisions, deciding what is important or trivial. It covers a vast field and the self is dependent on an intellectual ladder to climb over the obstacles of time.

Try convincing the intellect that almost all of its troubles are the result of the self-centred way it applies its energy and incisive grasp towards living and relating to others and the environment and the resistance mounts. The intellect is the pathway along which desires, likes and dislikes, all the particular inclinations and personal idiosyncrasies of the self are channelled in the search for fulfilment, satisfaction, comfort or whatever else the self is after. It takes up the psychological movements that arise, giving them verbal clarification, then points out the direction to go. The individual then acts in a conscious way to satisfy the moods, cravings, needs and demands of the self.

Deny the mind its intellectual outlet (thinking and reason) and it would probably go into shock. Via the intellectual storehouse, humans write, speak, receive and transmit ideas, acknowledge feelings, classify — oh, so many things can be done via this important storehouse of information. But it cannot create freshness, happiness, harmony or discover the spiritual Oneness, that universal nature that yields such a largesse of bountiful wellbeing with its discovery.

Without its storehouse the intellect couldn't function as it does. But to worship the intellect and its achievements above all else, to raise it onto a pedestal of the highest human endeavour is to court eventual disaster. It plays its finest role in the human expression when it is the servant of an enlightened mind, not the sole directive it aspires to be. The intellect does not foster love, cannot lead humans to God nor unveil the highest truths about human nature.

It builds bridges, cities, road systems and a million, brilliant technological marvels. It creates systems and organisations. But so too can it destroy what it has built. It can apply psychological techniques to enslave people within the societies it has fashioned. It has subdivided the human race into a multitude of divisions, nationally, socially, politically and religiously and set one faction against another in its desire for self-protection or domination.

Yes, many good things it has done but also much that is distressing and ugly. Take heed then, of its behaviour when it lacks spiritual discovery. Without this, there is a self-destruct button latent in the intellect. It begins to operate when the intellect goes too far in its intention to dominate the human race. It is inbuilt in the human psyche by the intellect acting in ignorance of its spiritual connection. Only love can defuse it, love and the truth released by spiritual awakening.

Until the advent of the spiritual the intellect does not even understand the nature of the self-destruct button nor how it activates it. The potential to destroy arises when it separates itself from its spiritual base and marches off on its own, bent on conquest via intellectual endeavour. This division from love immediately creates the self-destruct button and primes it ready for action.

The constant effort by the intellect to make self and its extensions more secure in the world of time makes the explosive power for disruption more potent. The longer the intellect defers the return to the spiritual fold, the greater the danger to mankind. Particularly nowadays when the destructive means available to nations through scientific ingenuity are so expanded by applied technology.

The intellect, in its bid for the survival and expansion of what it holds most dear has created the ingredients for worldwide destruction. It has skilfully devised pushbutton warfare and computer control of the weapons. Yet because of opposing social concepts and the divisions between nations, the security it craves still evades it. The tide of events threatens to sweep away its accomplishments when war threatens. Its response is to turn even more to its own resources, to its protective armoury to maintain its position — to the intellectual scientist for more advanced weapon systems and to the intellectual politician for complex arrangements that may preserve a precarious balance between opposing interests and permit it to go on its way in relative security.

For the intellect to continue building and acting without a spiritual directive in control is to invite deterioration individually and socially. What advantage is there for the intellect in a more intensive search amongst ideas and new inventions to safeguard its position and possessions if it does not understand the destructive bent that arises when the wisdom and love of a higher directive is absent? The means used to date have released widespread destruction at times. Fear of worse may perhaps have averted major catastrophes when crises intensify.

Every movement by the intellect in which a higher love and truth are absent must lead to confrontations with others and nature. The more complex the intellect, the more intense the confrontation and the more intractable the difficulties that follow. This is inevitable. Intellects that act divorced from spiritual light create fragmentation, divisions and an unbalanced approach to events and relationships. The vision of things must of necessity be self-centred, in which individual interests, or those of the nation are paramount. A universal outlook that appreciates the Oneness of humanity is absent.

Very few intellects will sacrifice the self in the service of a spiritual directive. Only those that are blessed with the understanding released by the spiritual will do so. The fear, the illusions, the desires that operate from within the intellect prevent its operation as an impartial instrument. The intellect cannot avoid the biggest pitfall of all and that is the level of its understanding and the limits within the thinking process. These create variable explanations to fit what surrounds it but in the end, what it deals with are ideas, logical outcomes and not realities as they are.

Everything is reduced by the intellect into thoughts, ideas and terms. This is for intellectual expedience. The grasping of ideas and concepts it does well and this is so much easier than approaching reality which is difficult to come by. I refer here to the Universal Reality. Awaken to this and the change in the intellect is profound indeed. This is a new direction to undertake, a lifetime one and one the intellect is unclear about so it prefers to stay in the troubled world it knows rather than venture where there are no definable stepping stones that it can use to support its very uncertain feet.

CONCLUSION

THE INTELLECTUAL MOVEMENT has been dealt with at some length in the hope this will instil a little caution in its use. The intellect will certainly do its best to avoid obvious dangers. But it is the hidden dangers, those not easily discernible to the perceptive power of the surface intellect that are the main concern. It is difficult to warn of dangers that cannot be clearly demonstrated through the use of reason. The intellect demands reasonable evidence before it will act on matters of consequence, otherwise it will continue much as it has done. Inner attitudes that may be detrimental to its wellbeing are something to be faced when the need arises.

What goes on in the depths of the human expression can only be appreciated when the voice of the intellect is still and not in an overriding role with its limited perspective. With this in a quiet mood, help may flood in from a higher source and this is what reveals the nature of the inner bent to generate the disruptive tendency that is latent in the intellect's movement. Whatever attitudes are fostered and supported inwardly, they must be brought out into the open so the intellect may see for itself the nature of this background control and where it leads.

The tragic human condition in many parts of the world is an obvious pointer to intellectual defects. Where is there harmony and happy togetherness — and for how long? The intellect is the instrument of technology, of organisation and the stronghold of experience and acquired knowledge. There is seemingly no end to the marvels that flow from the technological mind. However, the intellect has also engineered national enslavement and seduced vast populations with social propaganda.

People are effectively isolated behind political, religious, economic and racial barriers. Truth is often conveniently distorted to support the adopted standing. The universal oneness humans share in common without distinction isn't even a consideration let alone a reality in the lives of many. As pressure builds up due to the effects of the intellect's failure to align with the whole, feelings and violence are unleashed and run riot till the waves of destructive energy released are expended and some kind of stability temporarily returns.

There is unbalanced development in the world thanks to intellectual dominance. Those who have much reach out for even more while many starve and live in want. In some nations repression is rife, individual freedoms are suppressed and overriding the intellectual movement worldwide is the sinister propaganda of self-advancement, self-security, self-protection of the separate — economic gains, rights, ideas, traditions, whatever is the foundational base of the intellectual self. All this is initiated from group, state or national level as the intellect moves to strengthen its standing.

An overwhelming insistence is abroad in timeland to preserve the present status quo, to guard against changes that threaten the prevailing intellectual positions. The old ways are tottering, fractures are appearing in the complex social structures. They are based on separation, not on integration, on the self as a permanent fixture with the right to build as it will from this fallacy, not on the unified nature that is the reality behind the world of appearance. New voices, new ideas are breaking through the defensive armour of the old. The light of a new age is dawning and the intellect, immersed in the old ways is rallying to the defence of its position and accustomed way of doing things.

From a surface viewpoint it appears the decay and destruction has no interlinked purpose, no overall intent. Worldwide difficulties and violent outbreaks seem unrelated and the origins are considered the results of local and national differences. But the similar effects link the outbreaks together. They are indications the intellect, in its determination to deny the universality of mankind and maintain the fiction of separation with undisputed control of human resources to feed its appetite for psychological power and self-establishment, is bringing about results that do not vary much from place to place. The overall strategy is divide and subdivide — keep the underlying unity of the human race broken up into antagonistic segments, each suspicious of others and primed to self-defend at the least provocation. And attack and defend they do with all the savagery and cunning the intellects of today are capable of. And to hell with those men, women or children caught up in the middle of it all.

Discovering the Universal Oneness is not what the intellect is concerned with. It has created and identified with various political, social, national and religious ideas. It is dedicated to the preservation of what it considers its own systems. The consequence is conflict and dissension on a variable scale when opposing ideas fail to reconcile divergent standpoints. What profit is there in people fanatically supporting a complex of established ideas, even claiming freedom of choice as justification for what they do, if the end result is strife, aggressive postures and psychological pressure to gain their way? Such behaviour denies the essential unity of the human race which has its source in the Great Ocean of Being.

Instead of flowing like a placid river in time, in harmony with its timeless nature, there are many turbulent streams each urging to go their own way, pulling away from the mainstream movement of life. The stresses and strains that follow relentlessly unsettle the fabric of civilised societies. To the degree that they build up, mental, emotional and physical upheavals result.

As soon as the intellect patches up one area of breakdown, so another takes its place, and another as the confusion and misunderstanding inherent in the intellect's limited vision spreads ever outwards. With no spiritual directive acknowledged there is no overall bonding. The separatist human streams thereby flow in and out of confusion, conflict and discontent. Anxiety, despair and cynicism are some of the by-products of the human condition. All the negatives can only be dispelled by a realignment with the spiritual and the advent of the new light this releases to guide and infuse human living.

The intellects in control cannot do this for the people they supposedly represent. They too are under the influence of divisive and separatist attitudes and support these with all the weight of their logical reasoning. The individual intellect is likewise conditioned, not free to explore and investigate the total human content. But it can go as far as seeing that intellectual thought cannot lead to the highest truth or peaceful living while its approach is based on the false perception of separation and all that follows from this false premise. Sundered from its source in the spiritual Oneness the intellect is acting in a disjointed manner, is denying itself access to a higher level of understanding and is stagnating in time. The indispensable ingredients of love and togetherness are missing. Do what it will, organise differently, form new alliances, bring forth different ideas, yet still a free-flowing life on Earth will evade it.

An intellect full of its own self-importance, accustomed to being in control without deferring to a spiritual directive, is hardly likely to listen to words that suggest it is acting from a limited and self-defeating standpoint. Full of its own conclusions and offerings, knowing nothing of the spiritual, the assumption arises that intellect knows best what to do. It is, by inclination, bound to stay within the accustomed field it knows where it harvests the results of its inclinations and choices. It tends to disregard the role it plays in the troubles and problems it is caught up in. There is an insistence around, despite past failures, that with growing experience, additional knowledge and more time it can forge new arrangements that will protect its investments and attachments in timeland.

The intellect is the most optimistic, self-sustaining and self-indulgent of human activities and most prone to suffer delusions of grandeur, particularly when it operates in high offices of control and authority. Here it sees itself as an instrument of power, destined to do great things for humanity through the application of personal skills, intelligence and experience. It rarely questions the basis on which it forms its conclusions of self-worth but it carries on using the existing machinery of control, even rearranging this to make for an easier implementation of its intentions. So it goes its way imbued with the consideration that through its self-applied skills it has the necessary means to lead those reliant on it to a safer, more peaceful and prosperous life.

If the unfitness of the intellect as the sole directive is acknowledged, where then are humans to turn for the love, wisdom and understanding that is the only reliable guide for the human race? The human intellect operating from its accumulated background devoid of spiritual discovery has failed to be a worthwhile directive. It has yet to concede this on a worldwide scale. Technologically and in the field of organisation it is admirably suited to supply material needs. There is so much it does and supplies that make it indispensable to mankind.

But harmony, true peace instead of truces, bonding people together, eliminating corruption, intolerance and injustice, in all this it cannot proceed with technological skill and precision. Without this and love as its foundation to build on, its enjoyment of what it has created is disrupted by the uncertainty of human behaviour. Adults and children need the security supplied by love and peace to grow up in, to flourish. A happy atmosphere is necessary wherein violence and examples of violence are absent.

The intellect has failed to eradicate violence, selfishness and the unbalanced development of the human psyche. Many are reduced to living as limited expressions grasping for security through national, social and religious arrangements. Lifestyles saturated with shiny new possessions is often the main aim in life. Without possessions, mental and material, the intellect feels of lesser worth. There is an inner emptiness the intellect has failed to face. It prefers to supply distractions rather than go inwards, into the depth of what it is and face this emptiness, directly, simply, without complex intellectual explanations. Be one with it, not stay locked into separation.

In spite of national organisation and protective armour there is still insecurity and anxiety as to what may happen next. All the disorder is due to the intellect usurping its role in the human expression. It is responsible for the dispersion of mankind, for taking it way from its unified state, for gathering unto itself great power and authority and using this to further its own ends — the continuation of itself as separate and distinct according to its own interpretations. And it has failed to create peace and harmony, to look after and love humanity, which is what living should be all about.

Also, it has failed to spur the individual to reach for the divine nature within, to grow in spiritual understanding and walk tall as humans safely established in the universal. The intellect is stained with the blood of past and present misdeeds, has led mankind into many grave and destructive outcomes, two of worldwide ramifications in which it was brought face to face with the tragic consequences of misapplied energy, blind misunderstanding and devilish intentions.

The intellect can defend itself as it will from these charges but in the highest court of all, where the purposes and intentions of all intellects are known without self-distortion, spiritual truth and understanding pronounce these findings. There is a strange justice abroad. Here on Earth, as the intellect sows, so shall it reap.

So the consequences of its action inevitably boomerang back to bring home what has been so callously given out. The course of history confirms this. It is not a higher power that brings retribution but it comes through the intellect itself, in the way it reacts to aggression, to what it considers unjust, to unwarranted ill-feeling dished out. At the hands of the intellect, the intellect suffers yet it does not know the way of the strange inner laws by which it is brought to account for its deeds.

When the dark side of human nature is let loose with destructive intent, in the ensuing struggle that follows, everything the intellect is capable of doing it will do until the energy unleashed has exhausted its disruptive potential. Much as the dark side battles for supremacy and to continue its unpleasant characteristics, as the dust of each violent phase fades so the intellect has the chance to evaluate where it went wrong. Divine Love is always waiting to reclaim its human children. But the intellect must take the first steps to put aside its errant ways and return to its source in the Divine Strangeness. As the intellect signifies its willingness to do this by its awakening interest in spiritual literature and by initiating discipline to control what it can of its self-centred behaviour, so Love responds to help.

Enlightened ones will step forth on the human stage in greater numbers according to the interest shown. Should the former barriers to this new learning be put aside, the meaning will penetrate and evoke a response from within, from beyond the grasping intellect's range. As the awakening grows in intensity and intellect after intellect renews itself at the source of all, the new light released by the spiritual will gradually take hold. Love will blossom anew and lead mankind into life as it should be lived — free of self-created limits, of rampant ignorance and unbalanced behaviour.

Eventually the heart of mankind, unable to stand the separation from its spiritual homeland, must act to redress the imbalances caused by the intellect's rampage through time. When this happens and the return is effected in fact, the intellectual castaway, adrift in time's dream where it wanders without spiritual purpose, its true homeland completely forgotten, will awaken, not only to its true nature, but also to a clear realisation of the dark side of its nature. It will be washed clean of all stain and begin again to live, innocent and uncontaminated. Joy will walk this earth with love as its constant companion and the devious complications raised by fear, insecurity and ignorance, focused through the cancerous growth of the lesser self that prevails when spiritual truth is absent, will be no more.

Till that day dawns, my blessing goes out to you. We have all surely suffered enough.

Thank you for taking the time to read this book. Ratings and reviews are appreciated. If you enjoyed it, please Tweet/Share on your social media networks.

ABOUT THE AUTHOR

JOSEPH RAFFA WAS born in 1927 in Fremantle, Western Australia. He enjoyed an idyllic childhood roaming the bush and the seashore. In his teens Joseph became a dedicated atheist, looking to science for answers to the riddles of life and the universe. Then, in his early twenties, he experienced a moment of discovery that transformed his life. As Joseph's life opened out spiritually following this awakening, he was inspired to put pen to paper to encourage others to embark on their own journey of discovery.

Joseph died of cancer in 2010, leaving behind a legacy of inspirational writing which is now being made available to a wider audience.

Visit www.towardsthesilentheart.com for more information about Joseph and his books.

LOOK FOR OTHER BOOKS BY JOSEPH RAFFA

Beside Still Waters
ISBN 9780987227676

This beautiful collection of essays touches on the universal search for meaning and inspires readers to reach out for the still waters of the spirit.

The human heart longs for peace and harmony. It seeks a restful haven from the relentless busyness of everyday life, drawing us to spend tranquil moments in natural surrounds that offer a brief respite from the hustle and bustle. There is a state of inner stillness, when the endless chatter of the mind has ceased, that a deeper understanding arises. These are the 'still waters' that bring new life to mankind, that lay claim to the heart and redirect the mind. These are the waters of peace, love and true togetherness that lift us up to divine heights of being and living.

The Silent Guardian
ISBN 9780987227669

A timely reminder of our spiritual journey and true purpose on Earth.

Joseph shares an inspirational message for those who care to listen.

'Explore the planets, the outer reaches of space, the depths of the seas. Burrow into the earth, climb every mountain. When you have seen it all, you will still be left with the mystery of yourself. Turn and face this. Explore this. When you've travelled the extent and depth of the human expression, much of what you learn will be beyond the mind's capacity to convey through verbalisation. When heart speaks to heart, what more is there to say?' *-The Silent Guardian*

Beyond the Cross
The Christ Collection
ISBN 9780987227652

A moving collection of inspired pieces about Jesus.

Joseph Raffa was a dedicated atheist when he set out in search of answers to the riddles of life and the universe. Then, in a blissful moment of discovery, the God the Bible speaks of, the Allah of Mohammed and the longed for Nirvana of the Buddhists came into his life. As his life opened out spiritually, Joseph began to have a deeper appreciation of Jesus, His life and His role in the spiritual awakening of Mankind. Visions and insights arose unbidden, in such a manner that their authenticity could not be questioned. The young man who was an atheist for a time, who cared not to read the Bible or take much notice of Christ and His life, found himself anchored in God and also writing pieces extolling the virtues, the wisdom and the love expressed by that super spiritual being of long ago.